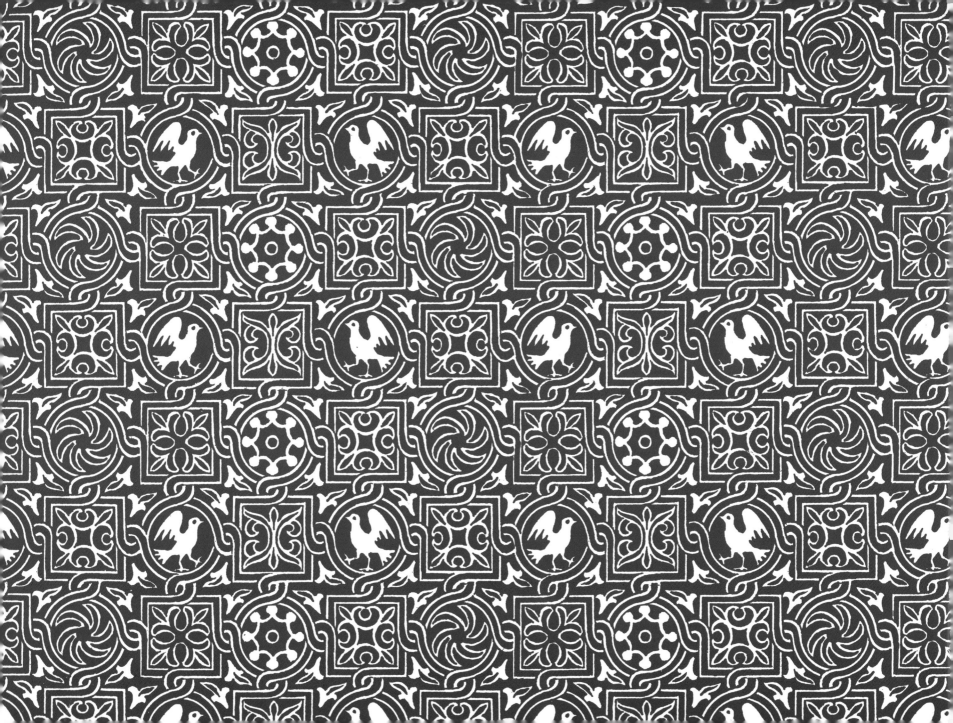

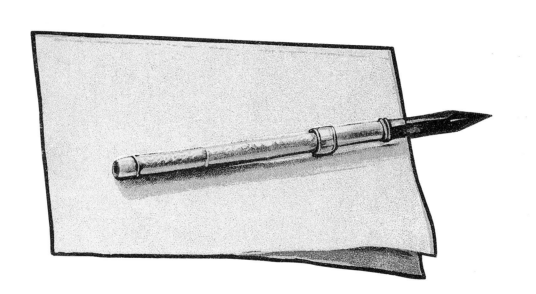

Writing Letters with *Pen & Ink*

EDWARD ST. PAIGE

DARLING & COMPANY   MMIII

ISBN 1-883211-59-X   FIRST PRINTING   ALL RIGHTS RESERVED   PRINTED IN SINGAPORE

DARLING & COMPANY   3645 INTERLAKE AVENUE NORTH   SEATTLE, WA.   98103

WWW.LAUGHINGELEPHANT.COM

All letters were written by hand until the invention of the typewriter in 1867. Even after that, almost all personal correspondence was handwritten, as typewriters were not available in most homes, and further, as *The New Standard Business and Social Letter Writer* explained in 1900, "In more intimate intercourse, the handwritten letter still reigns supreme. The mother does not want a machine-written letter from her son. Typewritten letters might be from some other son to some other mother. She wants to see her son's handwriting, for to her loving eyes, his angular, awkward, and even misspelt letters are a thousand times more beautiful and symmetrical than any letter any typewriter ever produced. What ardent lover would care to receive a type-written letter?" As the typewriter became more familiar and more available, it did intrude into the personal realm, and much correspondence was done with it, which led to a great increase of legibility. The personal computer, with its word processing capability, was widely owned by the mid-1980s and, because of the simplicity of correcting errors and moving sections about, attracted even more correspondents than the typewriter. It seemed to be the writing machine of our best dreams. The next blow to correspondence with pen and ink was email, which added the ease of instantaneous free delivery. Many people who had corresponded rarely using any of the earlier tools became verbose correspondents. Letter writing, which had been in decline, blossomed with this new invention, and communication poured out by the trillions.

What hope, in the face of all this, has the cumbersome method of writing letters on paper, with a pen, and then folding them into an envelope, placing a postage stamp on it, and carrying it to a postbox? I think this method has its uses and virtues, and this book explores them.

 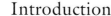

True, it slows one down to write it – and to read it. But in our so–called civiliza-tions, streamlined to the point of self destruction by the featherweight touch of a finger to a push button, we need to be slowed down.

—Irene Briggs Da Boll and Raymond F. Da Boll

Although it takes me longer, I write most of my letters to people by hand. I like the feel of it. I like the reminder of distance and separateness that the feel of the scratching pen provides. Often, too, instead of driving to the post office to mail them — and never mind that there are a thousand things I could be doing with the time — I take the extra half hour and walk. The to-do list gets longer, but never mind. I get an unexpected purchase on my thinking. I see things by the roadside. The world feels momentarily sorted back to its basic elements.

—Sven Birkerts

If economy of effort is the measure then there is no argument for penning one's correspondence. But we frequently ignore such rational behavior to our benefit. Why bake one's own bread when good bread can be purchased less expensively? Why grow vegetables when fresh vegetables can be pur-chased readily? Why struggle to learn to play the piano when player pianos do it for us, or CDs reproduce the playing of far more skilled pianists? We do these things because the doing of them is rewarding. The result is less important than the activity. Our loaf of bread is possibly inferior to that of one baked by a professional, but we savor it because of our effort. The car-rots we grow are probably small and twisted, but our effort makes them sweet. A simple tune played on a piano offers a satisfaction not offered by anyone else's playing. Mechanization has made almost everything easier, and has given us back much time we wasted in drudgery, but it has also taken away myriad satisfactions that come from doing, from making, from inserting oneself into a wide range of daily activities. We are in the luxuri-ous position, which our forbearers were not, of being able to choose from among the thousands of activities that machines do for us, the few that we would enjoy doing for ourselves, and to take them back because we enjoy performing them.

For me, writing letters by hand, with ink, on paper, is one of them.

Writing by hand, mouthing by mouth: in each case you get a very strong physical sense of the emergence of language ... print obliterates it, type has no drawl.

—William Gass

The anticipation of something arriving in the mail is, for many of us, a pleasurable aspect of daily life. As J.B. Priestly points out, it is not clear what is in the letter we wait for and no letter ever wholly satisfies the hunger. It is an aspect of what C.S. Lewis talks about in his book *The Problem of Pain*, and which he terms sehnsucht. This waiting, this yearning, this indefinable need is present in many aspects of existence, but nowhere as clearly as in our waiting for the mail. Most of us are not likely to receive unexpected cash awards, marriage proposals, or recognitions of our accomplishments in the daily mail, but we feel as if we might. As long as we hope, we open unfamiliar envelopes with excitement. Sometimes it does all come true, and our life is changed by a folded piece of paper in a stamped envelope. More likely the pleasures are more mundane – a letter from a friend or relative that tells us they remember us.

By penning letters to those we know or admire we add to the quality of their mail. We contribute a "real" letter to what is, in most cases, an assortment of bills and advertisements. We may not be able to fulfill most people's deepest yearnings, but we can touch their minds by having taken the trouble to write.

Life would split asunder without letters.

–Virginia Woolf

A pleasant letter I hold to be the pleasantest thing that this world has to give.

–Anthony Trollope

Especially in today's "I-need-it-in-a-nanosecond" world, there is something special about a letter sent, the treasures within. When we can fire off a memo into cyberspace without thinking, the act of writing a letter to someone is almost an occasion in itself. Indeed, the idea of "snail mail" as a way to bring us closer together is so quaint it's ... well, downright trendy. Do I hear a chorus of "Everything old is new again?" I hope so.

–Mary Alice Kellogg

Messenger of sympathy and love,
Servant of parted friends,
Consoler of the lonely,
Bond of the scattered family,
Enlarger of the common life

–Charles W. Eliot – Inscription on post office, Washington, D.C.

More than kisses, letters mingle souls;
For, thus friends absent speak.

–John Donne

Introduction

A phone call, an email, or a typed letter all demonstrate that we care, and convey our message. Why then my emphasis on writing letters with pen and ink on paper? The reasons derive, in part, from the rarity of the practice. In 1850 one would have not remarked the method of writing, because there were no alternatives. Now few letters are hand written and the recipient will certainly be aware that this was chosen over several alternatives. This evaluation, for most people, will be flattering. Faster methods, cheaper methods, easier methods, were all bypassed for this strange and old-fashioned practice. For the thoughtful this will be flattering. They will be aware of the effort spent and will understand that we think they are worth it.

Nothing gives greater pleasure than a letter penned by hand. Paper and pen still have their magic. We still entrust them with our dearest wishes and innermost thoughts and dreams.

—Kate's Paperie With Bo Niles

A letter never written or mailed has deeper significance than our merely being too busy. No one is too busy to tip a hat to someone he admires. We have to ask: "Busy doing what?" Whether it be a note to a friend whose son has been hospitalized, a woman who has just lost her husband, an eighth-grade English teacher who helped you improve your writing, a friend of your daughter's who is homesick on her exchange program from college — pick up your pen out of caring, appreciation, and love. It is never a burden to lift someone else's spirits.

—Alexandra Stoddard

I received a business letter today from a woman I do not know. The sender printed in small letters in a tiny hand. The ink was black. The capital letters were twice the size of the text, and were unusually distant from the rest of the word. The stationery was small, and several sheets were needed for a brief letter. It was embossed with a drawing of a little elephant. The envelope was rose colored, and it was addressed in white ink. The whole experience of opening and reading this was pleasurable, though a little difficult. Several things were obvious. First, the writer likes small and faint things, and has the courage to pursue her preferences. Second, she cares about the things that come from her hand, and is willing to exert herself to shape them. Third, she cared enough about the message to me to spend time and effort on it. She succeeded with me, as I think she would with most people. I read carefully, thought about her and her message, and wrote in return a longer and more carefully considered reply than I would have if her letter had been less striking. I have a similar inquiry from someone who sent it to me by email about ten days ago. I have not deliberately ignored it, but more pressing correspondence pushes it aside.

Do not lovers fondly linger, and dote, and dream over the very characters wrought by the hand they love so well? A letter from a lover's hand is a revelation that no machine—written letter can ever be. Besides all this, are there not dottings of i's and crossings of t's, and countless twists, and turns, and underlinings, all full to the brim of mystic meanings that no typewriter on earth could convey?

—Alfred B. Chambers

When a gift is given it is difficult to discern who is given the most pleasure – the giver who thought and shopped and spent, or the recipient who sees demonstrated someone's caring. So it is with letters.

Seemingly, the letter is a distant form of communication, but in actuality it encourages intimacy, for people frequently dare to write what they would find it difficult to say. Letters are kept, letters are destroyed, and letters are regretted because of this. A handwritten letter is the most intimate, for something of the writer's character and moods are revealed in the lines. Love letters are not simply a product of separation, a lesser form of intimacy, but are – in many cases – a central part of a blossoming affair, in which things are said that might not have been said otherwise. Lovers kiss their letters, put them next to their hearts. Surely letters of friendship are not as powerful, but they partake of the same revelatory quality – one person taking the care to stop in the midst of life and put their thoughts on paper.

Since his installation as bishop, he was known personally to pen all the letters of real importance to his diocese. How did he have the time, people inevitably wondered. Well, that was the whole point. He didn't. Which, of course, made his handwritten and reflective letters a treasure to anyone who received an example.

—Jan Karon

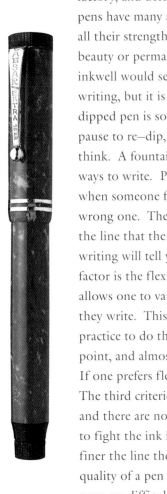

The choice of a writing instrument. There is much to say for a pencil. It is pleasant to write with, but the result is unsatisfactory, and deteriorates when handled. Ball point or felt pens have many advantages, and many adherents, and yet, for all their strengths, they cannot compare with ink writing for beauty or permanence. A pen which one must dip into an inkwell would seem to be a primitive and difficult means of writing, but it is not, and I often do it by choice. The fresh dipped pen is so full, and flows so easily, and when one must pause to re–dip, it provides a useful opportunity to stop and think. A fountain pen, if properly selected, is the best of all ways to write. Proper selection is not easy, however, and when someone first buys a pen they are likely to buy the wrong one. The first factor is the thinness or thickness of the line that the pen point makes. Only some experience in writing will tell you which line is best for you. The second factor is the flexibility of the pen point. A flexible point allows one to vary the thickness or thinness of the line as they write. This sounds desirable, but it takes a great deal of practice to do this properly. Most writers prefer a firm pen point, and almost all modern fountain pens are so equipped. If one prefers flexibility, antique pens are a better choice. The third criterion is the ease and steadiness of the ink flow, and there are no two views on this – no one wishes to have to fight the ink into the point and out onto the paper. The finer the line the more likely this is to be a problem. The last quality of a pen to weigh is ease of filling. Many fine old pens are difficult to fill, and this is a great frustration to one in the middle of a letter. The impatient filler may prefer a pen which uses cartridges of ink.

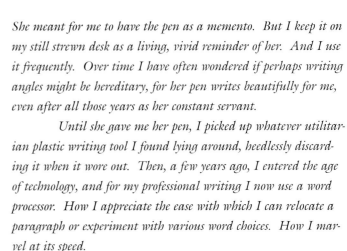

She meant for me to have the pen as a memento. But I keep it on my still strewn desk as a living, vivid reminder of her. And I use it frequently. Over time I have often wondered if perhaps writing angles might be hereditary, for her pen writes beautifully for me, even after all those years as her constant servant.

Until she gave me her pen, I picked up whatever utilitarian plastic writing tool I found lying around, heedlessly discarding it when it wore out. Then, a few years ago, I entered the age of technology, and for my professional writing I now use a word processor. How I appreciate the ease with which I can relocate a paragraph or experiment with various word choices. How I marvel at its speed.

But when the time comes to write a loving thank–you note, to compose a heartfelt letter of congratulations, or even to mark a special date on my calendar, I still reach for Mother's fountain pen, which waits patiently on my desk. As I begin to write, I feel a sense of graciousness and leisure that modern conveniences cannot provide.

Watching the point lay the glistening ink onto the paper, I feel compelled to do my best to make each circle perfectly looped, each letter permanently linked. Mysteriously, my usually scribbled handwriting becomes more like my mother's graceful script.

—Emyl Jenkins

Mother always dissuaded me from using her pen, telling me, "A pen point wears down into just the right shape for the owner. It won't write as well for anyone else."

—Emyl Jenkins

For five thousand years, the pen has been an indispensable tool of communication, lending a certain cachet to private, social, and business life. The fountain pen, which arrived on the scene only about a century ago, reached a peak of popularity and elegance during the 1920s, when it became a true status symbol, an expression of its owner's personality, social standing, and moods.

Replaced first by the typewriter, then the ball point pen, and finally the computer, fountain pens have only recently come back into style, thanks in part to an increasing affection and enthusiasm among collectors for vintage pens, and in part to the beauty and versatility that fountain pens lend to life's most important and personal moments.

—Alex Fortis and Antonio Vannucchi

Not only are the look of the pen and the writing different, writing with a vintage fountain pen feels different. The reason for the difference lies in the method of construction of the nib. Even a cursory glance will show that using a ballpoint pen offers no opportunity to impart character to handwriting. Modern pens that have a stub or a chisel–point nib can be used to create something of the effect achieved by a vintage pen. On down strokes, for example, such a nib will describe broad lines because the surface presented by the nib to the paper will be broad; on cross strokes the lines will be thin because the surface presented will be thin. However, the relative inflexibility of the nib will mean that there will be little variation between the thick and thin lines.

—Jonathan Steinberg

The Pen

There are times when my thoughts do not flow at all until I have dipped my pen in you. A drop of you helps me to think.

—George Aubrey Hastings

Ink should be bought in the tall, blue glass, quart bottle (with the ingenious non—drip spout), and once every three weeks or so, when you fill your ink—well, it is your privilege to elevate the flask against the brightness of a window, and meditate (with a breath of sadness) on the joys and problems that sacred fluid holds in solution.

—Christopher Morley

A GRACE BEFORE WRITING

This is a sacrament, I think!
        Holding the bottle toward the light
As blue as lupin gleams the ink;
        May Truth be with me as I write!

That small dark cistern may afford
        Reunion with some vanished friend,—
And with this ink I have just poured
        May none but honest words be penned!

—Christopher Morley

As with pens one must experiment with ink. Your favorite color may be orange, but orange is likely not to be the ink you will choose. Ink should flow readily, and should create an easily read result. I recently received a letter written in purple ink on gray paper. It was probably enjoyable to write it, but a strain to read it. Black is, of course, the king of inks, but some are willing to put up with the weakness of colored inks for variety. Even white ink has its place. Blue is the most popular ink color, presumably offering a compromise between the legibility and drama of black and the faintness of most colors, but it seems to me a weak choice. The frequent correspondent may choose to keep an arsenal of colored inks, and so match the color to the mood, the recipient, and most of all the paper.

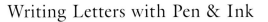

Namiki Blue

Campo-Mazio Noir

J. Herbin Rouge Caroubier

Campo-Marzio Seppia Caffè

Johnny Teal

J. Herbin Bleu Azur

Waterman Violette

Private Reserve Buttercup

Montegrappa 1912

J. Herbin Schiffgrüne

Campo-Marzio Bordeaux

Mont Blanc Brown

Pelikan Türkis

Rotring Ultramarine

Sheaffer Melon Red

Mont Blanc Ruby Red

Campo-Marzio Blu Notte

Johnny Grey

Sheaffer King's Gold

J. Herbin Vert Pré

Private Reserve Sherwood Green

J. Herbin Rose Cyclamen

Seppia

Waterman Black

Campo-Marzio

Campo-Marzio Grigio

J. Herbin Orange Indien

Yard-O-Led Claret

Ink

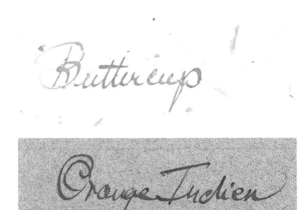

Despite the popularity of writing, stationery as we know it was unknown as late as the mid—nineteenth century. To answer a billet—doux, or love note, for example, a lady was obligated to trim a snip off a larger sheet of paper. The so—called trousseau of fine stationery is a Victorian innovation made possible by the Industrial Revolution and the ascendancy of the machine. The Victorians, notorious for governing every aspect of their lives according to the most arcane rules of etiquette, evolved a voluminous inventory of writing papers, which would be used at different times for different occasions.

—Kate's Paperie With Bo Niles

Not the only thing of importance, however, in a fine writing—paper is its superior texture and surface—finish. Color is also a factor which is paramount to excellence.

—F. Schuyler Matthews

Like so many choices, the choice of a writing paper is not simple. As with the selection of a pen or ink, experimentation is necessary.

White paper affords the most contrast, and for most colored inks is a necessity. Cream, which many prefer, offers, for me, a slight loss of contrast with no real gain (unless one is pained by stark white, which many apparently are). There are a myriad whites. Put against one another a selection of supposedly white sheets. You need to discover if your white is blue white, red white, yellow white, gray white, or so on.

The porosity of the paper is important. A very porous paper will absorb the ink and blur the lines. A very hard paper takes time to dry, and is thus easily blotted. The ink sits on the surface and cannot be as effectively manipulated as ink on a paper with a little receptivity. In choosing a paper one must position themselves along this axis of porosity and hardness.

Colored papers are dangerous. They change colors and reduce legibility. One some occasions, the choice of a colored paper, even a dark one, is worth the disadvantages. Here experimentation is absolutely necessary.

Papers with a heavily textured surface are unpleasant to write on. Paper with flowers, glitter, leaves, etc. embedded within are not reasonable surfaces for writing with ink.

The best way to know a good paper is to make one's self familiar with a great variety of paper.

—F. Schuyler Matthews

Paper

Ease up on the pen; make light lines
Free movement must be obtained F

The act of writing, if one is conscious of legibility, is a wonderful discipline. Our minds, which roil like captured oceans, are forced to order themselves and to send coherent messages through our fingers. The fingers must make small marks with care and precision. There are two reasons that so many people's handwriting is ugly and difficult to read. First, they have not been well taught handwriting in school. Second, they are in too much of a rush to discipline their hands. Even a poorly taught writer can be legible and distinctive if they will proceed with care and restraint, but in lives increasingly frantic this is difficult to accomplish. Writing is like yoga or Tai Chi; it forces our bodies to obey our minds. It encourages us toward harmony and deliberation. The best way to write is to determine to achieve an attractive and clear result for the sake of the reader. Love letters, or a letter requesting a favor, tend to be the most carefully written. We should write all of our letters with this much care, for the sake of our inner selves as well as for those who will receive and read them.

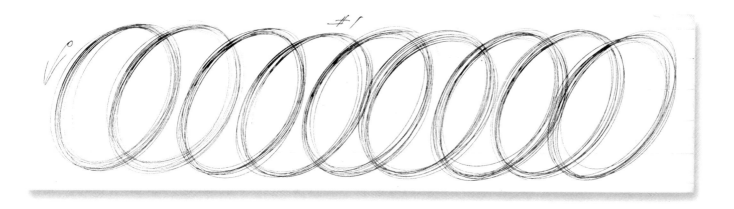

Further, the "hand–done" job invariably conveys a more heartfelt indication of personal regard & warmth where sentimental attachments are concerned, for instance, love letters & poems, marriage certificates, wedding & birth announcements – to mention such documents in their logical sequence.

There is no question but that the quality of American handwriting has fallen to a deplorably low level. This is evident with very few exceptions today, for everywhere we see handwriting that is notable mainly for its lack of legibility & penmanship. The reason for this is first, the lack of proper models & instruction in the public schools, and later, the disregard of any standard of legibility – let alone beauty – due most likely, to the prevalent urge to speed things up all along the production line.

—Irene Briggs Da Boll and Raymond F. Da Boll

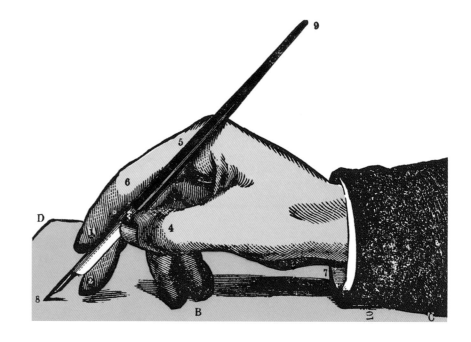

Personal lettering is the subtlest detector of one's substance and character; lettering is the scribe's confession, the score composed of his states of being, his impulses and his emotions – all the things that move him at the moment of communication. The scribe is subject to a rhythm that comes from his pulse, from the movement of his blood. A special kind of cardiogram, flowing and ebbing, a translation of invisible mental states into the visible. Each movement is a spiritual act and finds its appropriate symbol. Thus is lettering: royal and humble, vulgar and noble, muddled or freely structured and self–evident. A grand procession of all human conditions, bound together by the rhythm of a significant act.

—Friedrich Neugebauer

Machines have no grace. It cannot make a flourish, vary the thickness of a line, or tantalize the reader with a lapse into an indecipherable but lovely style. A good penman can make rivers that race to the sea, rivers as wild and dizzy as a flume in the Alps, as choppy as the Isarco, as wide and smooth as the Tiber at Ostia, or as deep as the Po where it rolls into the Adriatic.

But the so-called typewriter? It has attacked the holy blessed sap that binds all things. It is mine own executioner. Mechanized and quick, and dead as steel, like those guns that shot a hundred bullets at a time, it has killed my life, it has broken the beautiful lines, it has bullied and beaten time.

—Mark Helprin

 The Act of Writing

If the letter is going to be in answer to another, begin by getting out that other letter and reading it through, in order to refresh your memory as to what it is you have to answer, and as to your correspondent's present address

—*E.V. Lucas*

Many have trouble with correspondence. They wish to do it, they intend to do it, they try to do it, but there is a psychological barrier. For these people I make the following suggestions: Think of writing a letter as a physical performance, not as a test of your literary skills, but as thinking with a pen in your hand. Except in the case of a letter written to a new love, the recipients do not want us to be different than we are. They want communication from someone they know well. Their minds want to share our thoughts, and this is one of the best ways to do this. If we can discard our apprehensions, for this time forget our fear of failure, the words and thoughts will pour forth. Do not wait for the perfect moment when you are free of responsibilities and feel a rush of inspiration, but rather sit and write. You may start haltingly, you may take five minutes to write your first sentence, but stay with your open pen over the paper, and words will come. Sometimes it is like pumping water from a well. The first trickle is difficult to achieve, but is followed by a natural flow.

Speak with the pen! – that is what the best letter–writers do, whether they are literary artists, such as Lamb and Horace Walpole, Cowper and Keats, Edward FitzGerald, and Shirley Brooks, or the unknown pen–gossips whose letters are flying hither and thither at this very moment, linking household to household and heart to heart.

—*E.V. Lucas*

Let your letter be written as accurately as you are able – I mean as to language, grammar, and stops; but as to the manner of it, the less trouble you give yourself the better it will be. Letters should be easy and natural, and convey to the persons to whom we send just what we would say if we were with them.

—*Lord Chesterfield*

Arnold Bennet wrote a book called *Ten Minutes a Day* in which he asserts that brief, stolen moments, if properly used, can let you accomplish your unrealized goals. Certainly he is correct when it applies to writing. Trollope wrote his many, and lengthy novels, by rising an hour and a half early and writing. If you wish to be a regular correspondent simply devote some unused portion of your days to writing and you will be prolific. A little time before the practical day begins is perfect, but many other pieces of your day can be used. Television viewing is, to be generous, largely wasted time. Keep a pad and pen in your lap, and write during advertisements, or when you know what is going to happen. Ten minutes after dinner would be useful. If you ride public transportation, or are driven, write a little each trip. Arnold Bennet spoke the truth. The excuse that we haven't the time, which most of us use for one thing or another, is untrue. All of us waste time, and can gain it back through discipline. Writing letters to friends and relations is good for you and the recipients. Take the time to do it.

The complaint about letters is an old one. A century after the birth of Christ, Pliny the Younger wrote to his wife: "There is nothing to write about, you say. Well, then, write and let me know just this – that there is nothing to write about. Or tell me in the good old style if you are well." That is what all our friends and relations want to know from a letter – that we are well and thinking of them.

Feeling that we do not write very entertaining letters is no excuse for not writing to those who, as intimates, have a right to expect to hear from us. Write merely a line, as Pliny said, to tell "If you are well."

–The Woman's World Book of Etiquette

Write letters to friends and relatives very often. As a rule, the more frequent such letters, the more minute they are in giving particulars; and the longer you make them, the better.

–Thomas E. Hill

Imagine that you are lying on a hilltop, next to the friend to whom you would write a letter. It is a bright day, but with enough clouds to gentle the sun's rays. You look down on a wooded valley, and just beyond to a small town. You both lie silent for a while, enjoying the sun, the silence, the perspective. You speak.

Imagine that you have been skiing with your friend all of a long and wonderful day. You both sit on the floor of your lodge, in front of a burning fireplace, which provides the room's only light. You enjoy the flames for a long time in silence. Finally, you lie back and look at the shadows on the ceiling, and speak. At such time the heart opens. You can throw yourself into this mood without the hill, without the fire, without your friend's presence. If you learn to do this your letters will be good, and they will be enjoyed and valued.

Don't fill more than one page and a half with apologies for not having written sooner! ... Write legibly .... Don't repeat yourself ... When your letter is finished, read it carefully through and put in any 'not' that you may chance to have omitted.

–E.V. Lucas

Considering what a blessed thing the letter can be – and by letters I mean friend-
ly, intimate pen–chat – any method, however odd, is permissible.
Communicativeness is the grand test.

—E.V. Lucas

All of us undervalue the interest of what we see, think, and do. Imagine that you are a documentary filmmaker assigned to capture the essence of your life, your job, your day. This outside viewer sees the things that to us are too ordinary to be mentioned. The steady fall of leaves outside your window. The little rabbit that you won long ago at a carnival sleeping on a dusty shelf. The way you stand and stare at yourself in the mirror when you first arise. The torn kimono you use as a robe. The lovely swirl of cream into your hot tea. The awkward little girl who came to your door selling candy bars. The bird with yellow underwings. The bank clerk who acted as if no one before you had ever tried to make a deposit. The movement of a spider web on your room's ceiling. A man, who thinks no one sees him, making faces at himself in a plate glass window. A fellow worker, just returned from vacation, who won a huge jackpot at a slot machine and put it all back. The flower on your desk dropping its petals and pollen with great artistry.

All day long a wonderful world passes before us. We need only to see and tell of it to have the matter for a wonderful letter.

It's better to send several short letters than one enormous thirty-page effort ....
Don't wait for inspiration to come all at once. As events occur or when you read
something stimulating, jot down a quick note about it and keep the notes and clip-
pings with your writing paper. When you have a moment to write, you won't
waste time trying to remember what you'd intended to say. Visualize the person
you're writing to as if he or she were in the room with you.

—Sheila Ostrander

What and How to Write

With the advent of the new stamped envelopes there continued to exist for a time the old stampless, envelopeless, folded-letter packets with the amount of postage written or handstamped thereon. In fact, during the transition period of the 1840s and early 1850s, interesting admixtures of the two are found – envelopes with the old markings, folded letter sheets bearing stamps – as well as the occasional handmade envelope or the unique hand-drawn envelope.

Also during the early period of the envelope many methods of securing the flap were tried: sealing wax and wafer, of course, imitation wax seals, "motto seals," brass closures, and adhesive envelopes.

—Joe Nickell

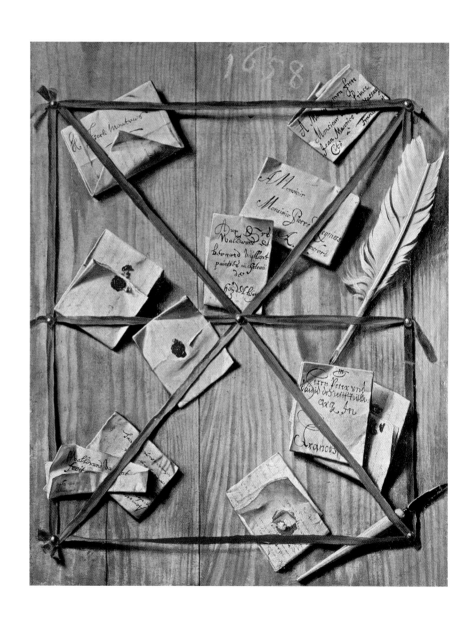

The custom of closing all ceremonious notes with sealing–wax is still adhered to by the most fastidious. It would be absurd, however, to say that it is nearly as common as the more convenient habit of moistening the gummed envelope, but it is far more elegant, and every young person should learn how to seal a note properly. To get a good impression from an engraved stone seal, anoint it lightly with linseed–oil, to keep the wax from adhering; then dust it with rouge powder to take off the gloss, and press it quickly, but firmly, on the melted wax.

—Mrs. John Sherwood, 1888

Envelopes convey a sense of mystery and anticipation .... The envelope is a triumph of engineering. When unfolded, an envelope resembles nothing so much as a paper airplane, but once doubled over on itself, it forms a tight, taut container that can submit to extensive handling as it makes its way to its destination.

—Kate's Paperie With Bo Niles

 Writing Letters with Pen & Ink

An envelope is one of the few things in the modern world we seal, thus creating a private space for expression.

—Thomas Moore

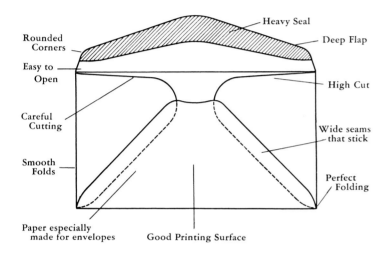

Rounded Corners — Heavy Seal
Deep Flap
Easy to Open
High Cut
Careful Cutting
Wide seams that stick
Smooth Folds
Perfect Folding
Paper especially made for envelopes — Good Printing Surface

The Perfect Envelope

Like their modern counterparts, ancient envelopes were intended to protect the documents they contained and to ensure confidentiality. Most materials used for the document itself — papyrus or parchment, for example — were also physically suitable for its wrapper, and would have been close at hand. The Babylonians even encased their cumbersome clay tablets in thin sheets of clay that were crimped shut and then baked ... the custom eventually developed of simply folding and sealing a letter in such a way that no outer wrapper was necessary. This was especially practical when paper was relatively expensive ... the use of envelopes was discouraged in England before 1840 by the fact that postal costs were assessed by the sheet. Any form of wrapper, therefore, "would have resulted in double postage being charged."

—Joe Nickell

Envelopes

Like a poet's rhyme scheme, or a minia-turist's ivory oval, the envelope decorator confronts an entertaining set of con-straints. The envelope is fairly small (usu-ally a rectangle). On it there must appear a legible address and a postage stamp. In this simple realm even the slightest visual touches are very noticeable.

—Richard Kehl

An archive of images of ruse in envelope garnishment can be built inexpensively by collecting pictures from magazines and advertisements. Thrift shops often have very inexpensive magazines. Photocopies of pictures in books are excellent when one needs a specific image.

—Richard Kehl

On the subject of stamps, let me stress that an array of stamps is a great assistance in making your mailings attractive. I recommend that you haunt your post office, stockpiling those with interesting designs. When the postal rates rise you may be left with stamps no longer useful for a first class mailing, but you can supplement these with more stamps of smaller denomination, sometimes overpaying the postage to achieve an exciting effect.

—Richard Kehl

TOP LEFT–HAND CORNER

| I CANNOT BE YOURS | DO YOU LOVE ME? | I SEND YOU A KISS | I LOVE YOU TRULY |

TOP RIGHT–HAND CORNER

| I AM ALWAYS THINKING OF YOU | I AM LONGING TO SEE YOU | WILL YOU BE MINE? | HAVE YOU FORGOTTEN ME? |

LEFT–HAND SIDE OF SURNAME

NO   YES

THE
LANGUAGE
OF STAMPS

RIGHT–HAND SIDE OF SURNAME

FORGET ME NOT

BOTTOM LEFT–HAND CORNER

| I WILL NEVER FORGET YOU | THIS AND MY LOVE | I AM ALWAYS TRUE TO YOU |

BOTTOM RIGHT–HAND CORNER

| DO WRITE SOON! | WHEN ARE YOU COMING TO SEE ME? |

I thank you for your easy flowing long letter (received yesterday) which flowered through me, and refreshed all my meadows, as the Housatonic – opposite me – does in reality.

—Herman Melville, to Nathaniel Hawthorne

As long as there are postmen, life will have zest.

—William James

I scan the mail for a hand–addressed envelope with an attractive stamp rather than an impersonal computer sticker on an envelope run through a postage machine. I crave letters from someone who knows me personally rather than someone to whom I am merely "Dear Madam or Sir," or "Dear Friend," a name on a mailing list or the person who pays the grocery bill.

—Alexandra Stoddard

And none will hear the postman's knock
Without a quickening of the heart.
For who can bear to feel himself forgotten?

—W.H. Auden

When I know that it is only about ten minutes from the usual time for a post, my mind refuses to concentrate on any other matter; I pretend to read or write, or try to get up a brisk passage of talk, but it is all a hollow pretence; I listen for every footfall. I am as foolish as a young lover awaiting his adored, without – alas! – his divine excuse. It is a pitiable farce trying to do anything else when every nerve in my body is crying out for the familiar rat–tat at the door and the comforting clop–clop of the falling letters.

–J.B. Priestley

We always expect good news and cheques; and then, of course, there is the magical Fortune which is coming, and word of it may reach me any day. What it is, this strange Felicity, or whence it shall arrive, I have no notion; but I hurry down in the morning to find the news on the breakfast table, open telegrams in delighted panic, and cry, "Here it comes!"

–Logan Pearsall Smith

I'm feeling better and better and a letter from you from time to time would foster my recovery; don't be too stingy.

–Édouard Manet

Who was the woman who once declared that she was only prevented from committing suicide by the fear of missing the next post?

—J.B. Priestley

  23   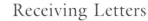 Receiving Letters

I have walked on air all day since getting your letter.

—Vita Sackville–West to Virginia Woolf

If letters did not exist, what dark depressions would come over one! When one has been worrying about something and wants to tell a certain person about it, what a relief it is to put it all down in a letter! Still greater is one's joy when a reply arrives. At that moment a letter really seems like an elixir of life.

—from The Pillow Book of Sei Shonagon

A short time ago, my posts had dwindled almost to nothing and I was becoming uneasy and suspicious, indeed, not untouched by misanthropy; so I decided to go away for a week or so, ostensibly for a rest and a holiday, but in reality (for I had given orders that no letters should be forwarded) that I might have the pleasure of handling a large number of letters all at once when I returned.

—J.B. Priestley

Letters give life a rich dimension. They can be saved, savored, reread and treasured for hundreds of years.

—Alexandra Stoddard

I have taken refuge in the theory of the One Supreme Letter, of which all others are but the shadow. This it is what we expect knowing nothing of what it will contain, or of what form it will take, but only feeling that this Letter alone will completely satisfy this strange craving of ours.

—J.B. Priestley

You said yourself you would not be able to write.
Reckoning up your halts for eating and sleeping —
By this time you've crossed the Shang mountains.
Last night the clouds scattered away;
A thousand leagues, the same moonlight scene.
When dawn came, I dreamt I saw your face;
It must have been that you were thinking of me.
In my dream, I thought I held your hand
And asked you to tell me what your thoughts were.
And you said: "I miss you bitterly,
But there's no one here to send to you with a letter."
When I awoke, before I had time to speak,
A knocking on the door sounded "Doong, doong!"
They came and told me a messenger from Shang–chou
Had brought a letter, — a single scroll from you!
Up from my pillow I suddenly sprang out of bed,
And threw on my clothes, all topsy–turvy.
I undid the knot and saw the letter within;
A single sheet with thirteen lines of writing.
At the top it told the sorrows of an exile's heart;
At the bottom it described the pains of separation.
The sorrows and pains took up so much space
There was no room left to talk about the weather!

—Po Chü–I

Receiving Letters

Between these two drawers is a recess into which I throw whatever letters I receive. All that have reached me during the last ten years are there. The oldest of them are arranged according to date in several packets; the new ones lie pell–mell. Besides these, I have several dating from my early boyhood. How great a pleasure it is to behold again, through the medium of these letters, the interesting scenes of our early years, to be once again borne back to those happy days that we shall see no more!

—Xavier de Maistre

I've been to 70 countries to date and sent Aunt Marie a postcard from every one. I know now how much she treasured those tiny messages, sent from places she would never see. And when I journey through my correspondence hat box, I know that nothing can replace the treasures within. Posed as we are at the beginning of a new millennium, it will always be the thought sent and saved that counts the most in the heart.

—Mary Alice Kellogg

Writing Letters with Pen & Ink

Letters are one of the most tangible memories of our friendships, and we should save them as we save photographs, and other personal mementos, so that we can evoke past friends and vanished times.

—Edward St. Paige

Each life is unique, and yet the exact flavor of personality is made up of many small things which are sometimes difficult to evoke. It helps to have a person's thoughts and words as an aid to our memories, and thus saving the letters of those we value is a way to give deeper reality to our lives and theirs.

—Welleran Poltarnees

When the spirits sink too low, the best cordial is to read over all the letters of one's friends.

—William Shenstone

Letters have a way of pinpointing the moment. We tend to describe the setting, what we are wearing, the weather, what we ate for lunch, what music we're listening to, our reaction to the current political situation. Rereading old letters can remind us where we once were physically and emotionally at one very specific time in our lives. When my mother died, I discovered she had saved most of the letters I had sent her, beginning when I was nine at camp in Maine.

—Alexandra Stoddard

FOUNTAIN PENS

There are many useful books on pens, all well illustrated, but I have found most useful this brief inexpensive volume:

Fountain Pens, by Jonathan Steinberg.   Universe Publishing, New York, 2002.

INK & PAPER

There is little practical use in reading about ink and paper choices, but if you enjoy as I do, finding written words to fit every situation, I send you to these two books:

Paperie: The Art of Writing and Wrapping with Paper, Kate's Paperie with Bo Niles. Simon & Schuster, New York, 1999.

This is a book about using paper, and thus casts its net much wider than the scope of my book, but it does proceed from a real love of paper and what can be done with it.

The Writing Table of the Twentieth Century. By F. Schuyler Matthews, Brentano's, New York, 1900. (Out-of-print)

Too much of this curious volume concerns heraldry, but when he talks about paper, Matthews displays knowledge and taste.

HANDWRITING

All of the recent books that I have found teach calligraphy, lettering, or italic handwriting. These are fine disciplines, and if you want to master them there is ample help available, but what interests me is improving and disciplining one's ordinary handwriting through exercise and example. The best

books I have found that do this are old and out–of–print, but they, or ones like them, should be discoverable in used bookstores or websites:

Palmer's Penmanship Budget by A.N. Palmer and C.J. Newcomb, New York, 1915.

A useful and detailed work on good handwriting which was used by the widespread Palmer Method as a textbook, and printed many times.

Real Pen Work, Pittsfield, Massachusetts, 1881.

An instruction book for beautiful penmanship, with detailed lessons and inspiring examples.

CORRESPONDENCE

The Victorian age enjoyed guidebooks to letter writing, which suggested wordings for many possible letters. They can be useful when inspiration is low:

The New Standard Business and Social Letter Writer, by Alfred Chambers. Laird & Lee, Chicago, 1900.

A typical work of its kind. This, or one of many like it, should be easy to find in a good used bookstore.

The Someone Cares Encyclopedia of Letter Writing. Prentice Hall, Boston, 1997.

A modern version of the above, which gains by using more contemporary language, and loses in quaintness.

Picture Credits

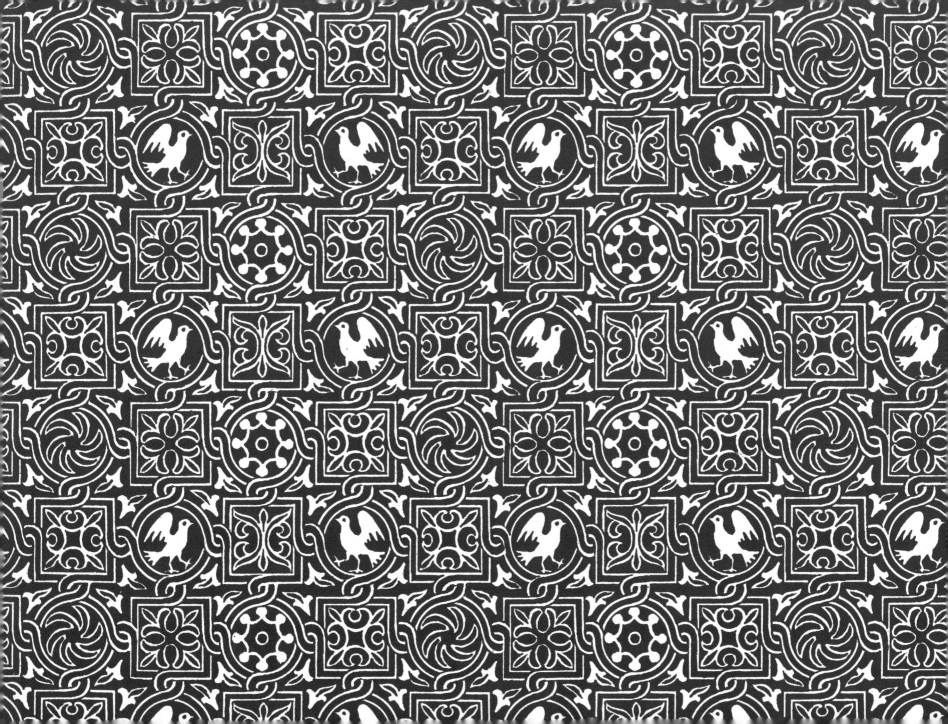